T0198778

Horrid Jokes II

Alexander Galica

....For Cookie Wilson....
....And Robert Wunning....

Wibbling-Ooglina
(The sun always shines on T.V.)

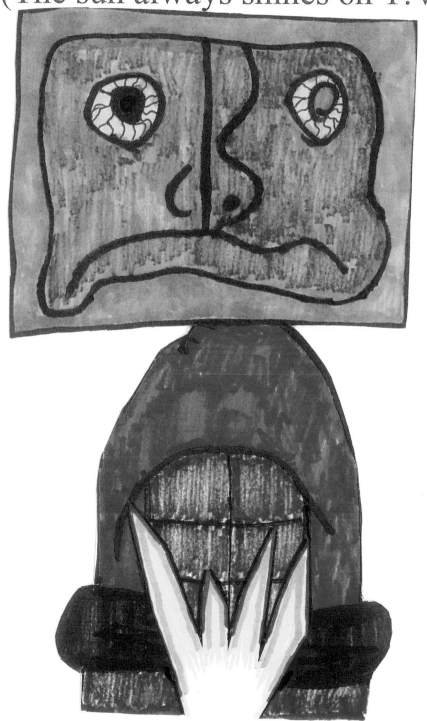

O no .I can't get my pants down!

Guess what?
I won a Gold-Fish at
the Fayre.
And Daddy flushed it
down the JON.

O you really are…

..The Kiss of Death.

WOMAN – Were you dropped on your head as a baby, crash, bang, wallop?

MAN – Dour bisher `No you mucked my head up and threw me too the wolves!

WOMAN – And how did that make you feel?

MAN – Slimy worms too the lot of them .Except you, you're a ruddy man-eater.

WOMAN – Sank you very much (she said) .Rather sarcastically too in the end!

Mister Fish-Mister and Mister and Mrs Ba-boomp there. Thank you please.

Greystoke

Tarzan lord of the jungle .He could talk too all the animals.

One day an expedition happens upon him .And they take him back to the West .Where he gets wined and dined and women .And generally lives in the fast lane for a while .

When he suddenly decides he wants to go back to the jungle .Where he thinks he belongs really .But when he gets back to the jungle .None of the monkeys know what he was on about.

`Except Tarzan (one of them chirps up) .If you are living in a hot country .You must stop drinking from the furry cup!

.Tarzan-Returns.

Tarzan was in a filthy mood
about something one of the
monkeys had told him.
`What are these bloody
straws doing in the Jon? `
He snapped angrily.
`Go & throw yourselves in
the river at once…
if you are all feeling so
damn thirsty…
and I hope you f-in well
drown! `……………….
And he would not apologise.
And he did not care either?!

Douglas Heard ate some curd and did a turd, silly old Douglas Heard.......?

JAWS.

There was an Englishman.
An Irishman.
And a Scotsman.
And they all go shark fishing in a
rowing boat.
But they are not catching anything.
So the Englishman says to the
Scotsman for a joke `Why don't we
throw the Irishman overboard
perhaps we might catch something! `
Ha ha ha they both chuckle.
But the Irishman overhears them.
And he turns on the other two!
`I know` he says `Why don't we
ALL go for a swim? `
Ba-Boomp he capsizes the little
boat. Drowning them all in the end.

The Wrong Number

666 the man hurriedly dialled the number .

He was reading it upside down .

He thought he was calling the police to say `that he had had the most terrible accident",

`He wasn't sure if he had had an accident or not but was getting more and more confused by the second ,could they please come at once?"

In three flicks of a lambs tail a car arrives and the man is promptly arrested on the spot !

`I can't see where

concerned th

something?

`Were

all day

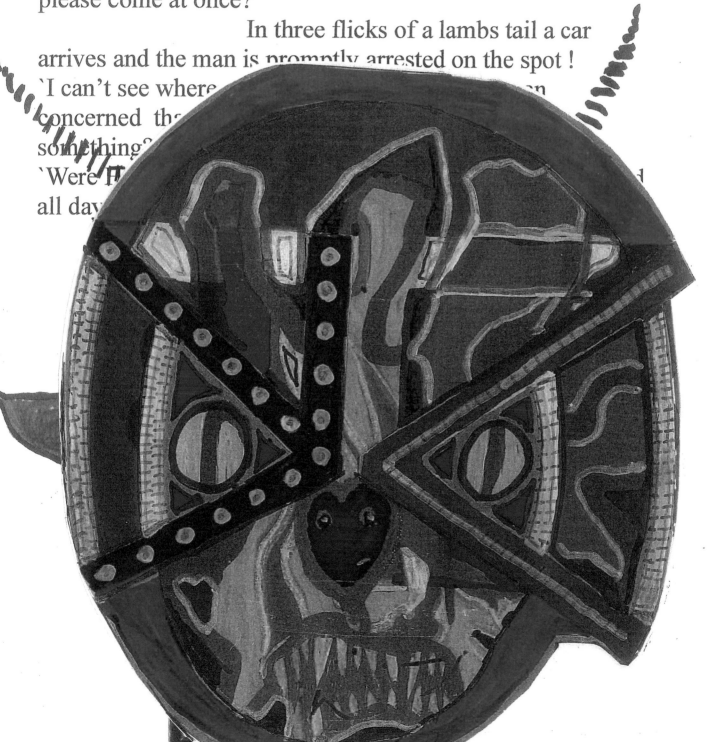

John the Bunny....And the Banana Smoothie

Deters ear's hurting \<Er-Ting-Kirk-Inn-Tuts\> not feeling very Well.\<Well\>John the bunny flew down the stairs at Z speed of light ,with the banana smoothie!
`Drink this" he said very persuasively
`Drink it" he was absolutely convincing
`DRINK" this time he was very firm
& I drank the thick yellow liquid down , it tasted caustic/tainted like a powerful cough mixture or forbidden fruit or a banana smoothie from the future or something and as it loosened my palette (dear friends) ,all of my feelings seemed to wash away and I felt very sleepy.
`Good ,that's done the trick?"John the bunny said
`Now we can all go up too bed & not go out & paint the town red ,after all ,who wants to anyway?"
`Alley.....Rue...Deter.....anyone else...........................?"
& In The End everyone did ,because you want the best for your children?..................

.Ancient Chinese proverb.

A woman and a cow both give milk. But if you are thirsty get it from the cow?

…The laughing cow!

Melody's Milk Bar

Melody was terribly busy today ,it was early morning ,soon the people would be here & she had a lot to do.
Melody's milk bar was famed for having the most fabulously tasty milks in the whole land and people came from far and wide to enjoy them............
One of the things she had to do before anyone came every day was mix up all the different flavoured milks .She did this every morning and had got it down to a fine art .
Some of the best-selling drinks the milk bar sold in descending order

1. Peach Melba
2. Orange & Lemon
3. Raspberry Ripple
4. A Tangerine Dream
5. Strawberries & Cream
6. Banana & Toffee
7. Coffee & Chocolate
8. Mint Chocolate Chip
9. Butterscotch
10. Mango Madness

(O all made with milk of course)
These were her most popular drinks and apparently they were very very good indeed .There were other good ones although their recipe was a secret (some of them were very hush hush).

IA The END

.FARMER STRAW-BERRY`S PINK FARM.

You must never give On-ken that many peas .I mean he could not do any more if he tried .You know what I mean .It is as dangerous as it is stupid .And furthermore it is quite inconceivable too ,as a matter of fact .I would not do it .Who would try it for starters?

Anyway a peculiar look entered On-kens eyes .When he realised, they were going too try and send him round the twist! And it was that day he swore .He would have them all.

They gave him nothing the following day .Because he was expecting a load of peas and whack and smash <Too soften him up and make him more cooperative, easier to manipulate and generally weaker>.

And guess what? He didn't get a sausage!

But that was normal .They never did anything normal On-ken mused (Ho hum).

The real test of sanity came later the next day .Actually it was Satan's baby. `I hope you roast in hell you porker` the Devil had taunted.

The Devil was going too enjoy this .Enjoy it .And then perhaps have some sausages at the end of the day .All going well .It was all good!

Little did the Devil know that On-ken was not a piddle-e-art .But a young-n in the transition between a boy and a man?

On-ken would never become a real man .You see unless he could resist the temptations of the Devil .And all evil. On-ken had once foolishly let it slip .That one day he wanted too be a man more than anything.

And the Devil had overheard him.

And that was why On-ken was being punished by the Devil so severely .And also in the slightly hazardous predicament of going too slaughter with the other swine! But he was a brave boy and he wasn't suddenly about too loose his marbles.

You see you could never do anything too On-ken .Unless you had him around your little finger .And that was how you got him. But no one knew this.

If you did a proper job on On-ken .If you beat him. Then he would mutate. And become a dirty, piddy beast.

And if that happened On-ken would be cursed forever as a little boy and never be able too grow up and become a man .More importantly he would never be able too perform his destiny .Too rid the world of the Devil and all evil. {He was the chosen one apparently born too do this}.

However our hero On-ken .Now tipped off too what they were trying to do to him, was pumped full of peas and whack and smash .And sent packing .Off to Satan's Sausages!

<If he got a duff one he was stuffed>.

Too give the butcher a fiver and tell him what he knew, if anything at all?

{How did On-ken escape the butcher's hungry jaws?}

Well when the butcher had asked what he was.

On-ken had lied!

And said he was just a dog.

And the fiver was for some sausages for his master……

…………I think the real message going out here is.

We all have a cross too bear against evil .And evil things .And it might be the only thing we have .But we still have it.

Anyway Six Hundred and Sixty Six pounds worth of sausages later (Rather a lot of pork, don't you think).Farmer Strawberry's been fired!
And the Pink Farm, well that's another story…………..

.The Medusa Circuit.

<Phase.1.>.Inner-sense.

No disintegrations.

No drivelling
vegetables.

And a mess is not
allowed.

.The Medusa Circuit.
.(Phase.II.).The Paw.

...EAT THE RICH.

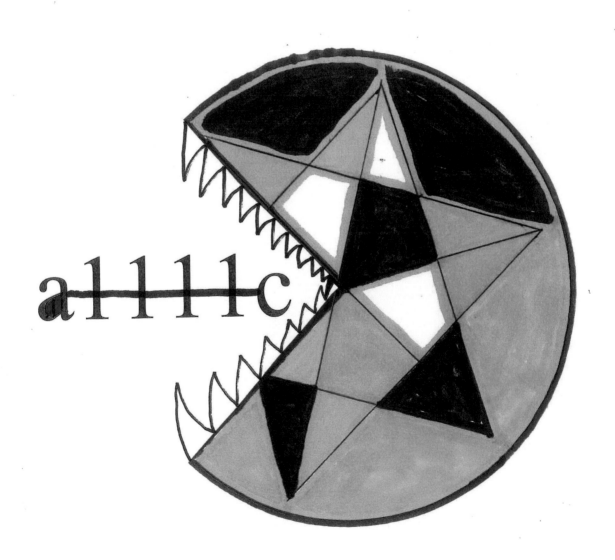

.... If 6 were 9

& 9 - 6......

The Medusa circuit.
<Phase .5.>Final Conflict.

Mankind's eternal power struggle between the forces of Good and Evil.

.The Medusa Circuit.
<Phase.6.6.6.> .True Love.

An old wise guy once told me the answer to everything. `The greatest thing you will ever know" he said `is just too love and be loved in return". So it was a bit unfair he got the D* hat for telling me.

*Dunces

The Medusa circuit.
<Phase .7> .Freedom.
.1234567.

Well anyway I have
ceased too exist.

I have gone
completely mad.

And I have badly
crapped my pants.

.Twelve No Brainers.

I was feeling a little bit tired, so I went too sleep.

That doesn't mean that, that does.

O well I am just wondering now.

Anyway you can if you want, but you don't have too.

And apparently carrots can make you see in the dark and everything.

Malfunction – I am not going to work today.

And Paul's been damn rude as well.

Don't play with fire or you get burned in hell.

It was raining and we got wet.

I live in a house.

Sweeties are really quite nice actually, sweeties are.

And the cows are in the field eating grass and things.

Rock`N`Roll

.Manhood.
A Little boy
runs up a hill.
And comes
down a
mountain.
Fully grown
up. Ali .G.

If it is the
word that
calls for
change?
Your shit out
of luck!

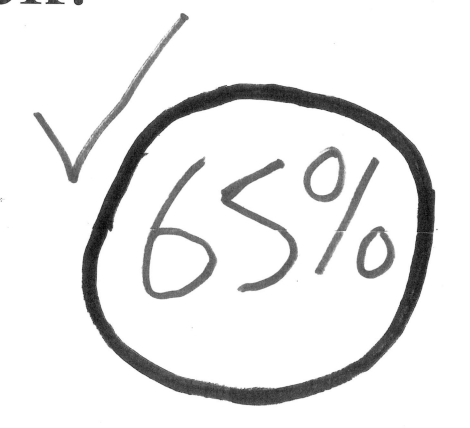

The Poisonous Fish

If you see a poisonous fish,
do not look at it,
do not step inn-it,
do not go near it,leave it alone,
do not try and eat it,
do not try to sit next to it,
do not go soppy on it & try and kiss
it, do not French kiss it,
do not try and chat it up or be its
friend ,
show it no mercy ,for you shall
receive none,
do not film it ,or snap it or try and
put it in your family album,
do not tell everyone about it,
keep your mouth shut,
and whatever you don't look at it ,
,and don't step inn-it!

Go Bananas 4

Mummy Na Na used to tell her little Narnies not to leave their skins lying about or Mr Socks would get them!

So they were always a bit careful when they got a Banana in the........Na Na Ne Na Na ? End

Suddenly Mr Socks appears to give some nutritional info on the value of bananas and how very good they were for you.

But ,shock horror as the bananas were running for it..............................One of them has gone flying on the poisonous fish.Luckily however the other one splits...................................

.Doctor no.2.

`Doctor, doctor I think I am pregnant` said the man
`You cannot be serious` said the doctor
`Whoppers` said the man
`I am absolutely full of it, I am absolutely full of shit` roared the man
`Shush quieten down` the doctor said `You're scaring my patience`...Ha ha BONK

.Doctor no.1.

`What time is it? `
Asked the man
`It is nearly a quarter
2 – 1 `replies the
Doctor
`O my god I have too
go now doctor` the
man said `Can I go
now or not` said the
man defiantly?

`Get out of here` said
the doctor angrily
`At once`
It's not a quarter 2 –
1 yet is it `asked the
man again slowly
<Dead Pan>
`No its not, its not`
replies the Doctor
`It's all over my
carpet! `

.At Last.

I went down too the bank
the other day.
And I ask to borrow some
money.
`We are ever so sorry - but
we have given it all too John
the Bunny` .They say..........
`What have you done that
for`? I ask........................
`Because we don't want you
to have it`! They say..........
Gotcha fuckers, now I know
at last - INNIT.......... The END

(Horrid Jokes II)

(Horrid Jokes II)

You do as much as you can.
And then you take from it
what you need.

Alex was born in Wiltshire
England .And studied
English at school .He is also
a recognised Artist and
Musician .He now lives a
quiet life as a writer and
poet.

AuthorHouse™ UK
1663 Liberty Drive
Bloomington, IN 47403 USA
www.authorhouse.co.uk
UK TFN: 0800 0148641 (Toll Free inside the UK)
UK Local: 02036 956322 (+44 20 3695 6322 from outside the UK)

Because of the dynamic nature of the Internet, any web addresses or links contained in this book may have changed
since publication and may no longer be valid. The views expressed in this work are solely those of the author and do
not necessarily reflect the views of the publisher, and the publisher hereby disclaims any responsibility for them.

Any people depicted in stock imagery provided by Getty Images are models,
and such images are being used for illustrative purposes only.
Certain stock imagery © Getty Images.

ISBN: 978-1-6655-8987-1 (sc)
       978-1-6655-8988-8 (e)

Published by AuthorHouse 05/27/2021

authorHOUSE

Printed in the United States
by Baker & Taylor Publisher Services